Contents

1. What are presentation skills?

For most of us the idea of standing up in front of a group of people and speaking at length on a complicated subject (or any subject) fills us with complete fear. Death by slow torture seems preferable.

Nevertheless, presentation skills can be learnt. By thorough preparation and practice you can equip yourself to meet the challenge. Think about a comedian preparing a stand-up routine. He or she will spend hours and hours researching material, testing jokes and delivery, and practising in small clubs or pubs. Eventually on stage the performance seems effortless – and fun to do! But that 15-minute slot represents just a small percentage of the time spent preparing a seamless routine.

As a communication tool, live presentations have far more impact than a report or telephone call. They can make complex ideas or arguments easier to understand and remember, by combining visual stimuli with speech. Remember the last television weather report you saw. In a few seconds, with some clever computer graphics and clear language, the presenter explained varied weather conditions and changes over time.

All the details are important – what you say, how you say it, how you look and move, the supporting props, and the organisation of the room itself. They all contribute to the impression each member of the audience gets, and how well you deliver your message.

Why are presentation skills important?

Presentations are used to inform, persuade, motivate, instruct or change people's attitudes or ideas. There is normally a business purpose – you want the audience to do something as a result of listening to you.

The ability to stand up in front of groups and talk effectively – so they understand your message and are prepared to take the action you want – is crucial for a successful business career.

Here are some examples of typical presentations:

❑ A speech at a conference
❑ A press briefing
❑ A department meeting on plans for the next year
❑ A proposal for a new project to a board or committee
❑ A retirement speech
❑ A sales presentation to a potential customer
❑ A training session on new computer software.

Good presenters talk with confidence, develop an empathy with their audience and use all the elements available to them to deliver an effective message in the time allotted. When you have got a group of people together they aren't doing any other parts of their jobs – so it's important that their time isn't wasted, and the purpose of the presentation is achieved.

How do I stop being nervous?

'The human brain starts working the moment you are born, and
never stops until you stand up to speak in public.'

Sir George Jessel, 1949

Why are we afraid of standing up in front of people? It boils down to
being frightened of looking foolish and being laughed at, or not being
liked. Yet we all know that embarrassment is not a terminal disease,
however uncomfortable it feels at the time.

So think about what can go wrong in giving a presentation – what are
you scared might happen?

- ❏ Your voice dries up
- ❏ You start to stumble and stutter
- ❏ Your mind goes blank
- ❏ Your notes get mixed up
- ❏ You use the wrong words accidentally
- ❏ The audience doesn't understand what you are saying
- ❏ The slides get mixed up
- ❏ You fall over
- ❏ You don't have enough to say
- ❏ You run out of time
- ❏ The equipment doesn't work
- ❏ No one can hear you
- ❏ People stop listening and talk to each other
- ❏ You get interrupted or asked a question you can't answer
- ❏ A fire alarm goes off, and the building is evacuated.

Apart from the last event (which you might secretly hope happens!),
preparation and practice can overcome all of the other gremlins. Decide
what you are worried about, and work out ways to deal with the
potential problem.

Remember that the audience is not just there to laugh or hiss at you.
They may attend for a variety of reasons, and some may not want to
waste the valuable time in their day, but if you have something useful to

say, you can make them interested and teach them something. So think about the purpose of your talk – to share information you have with people who could benefit from knowing it.

Preparing yourself psychologically is important, but much more fundamental is getting the practical aspects right. So you will need to think about and work on the following elements:

- ❑ establish your objectives
- ❑ find out about the audience
- ❑ decide the content and structure
- ❑ prepare notes
- ❑ prepare visual aids
- ❑ practise and get feedback
- ❑ get the room right.

If you know you have all the basics right, you will have more confidence in your ability to get your message across. Then you will be able to give a fluent and informative presentation without embarrassing hiccups or distractions.

2. How do I prepare the content of a presentation?

How do I set objectives for a presentation?

Like all forms of communication, presentations need thorough preparation if they are to be effective.

Why are you giving a presentation at all? You must be clear about the objective of the presentation, because that will determine the content and structure of what you say.

Aim	The presentation should...
Provide information or background	Inform people or describe something – provide facts and details. For example, describing the outcome of a research study on your company's customers.
Instruct or explain	Show how things work, and why they are organised the way they are. For example, an introduction to computer systems for new members of staff.
Persuade or convince	Give an argument for the audience to change their ideas or behaviour. For example,

	requesting approval for a project, or getting a customer to buy your products.
Entertain or amuse	Be relevant to the audience, and combine information and humour. For example, an after-dinner speech, or a leaving presentation.

When you have worked out the aim, focus the detail and set objectives for your presentation that are SMART:

Specific
Measurable
Achievable
Realistic
Timed

Here are some examples:

'To get the directors to approve a budget of £20,000 to provide new uniforms for security staff within a week.'
(Depending on your company's financial status that may or may not be realistic!)

'To get all department members to use a new voicemail system, so that by the end of the month administrative staff only handle urgent calls.'

'To inform all employees about the company's financial performance, so they understand the need to monitor costs.'

Once you have established what you want to achieve – and that your objective meets the SMART criteria – then answer some practical questions…

❏ **When** will the presentation take place?
❏ **How long** will it be?
❏ **Where** will it be given?
❏ **Who** will or should be there?
❏ **How** will it be delivered?

…before getting started on **what** should be covered.

How do I get it right for the audience?

Find out about who you will be speaking to. What do they know already? What are they particularly interested in? What is relevant to them? What do they expect you to say? What benefit are you offering? What will persuade them to change their minds or behave differently? On the flip side, what would they be bored by? What would be irrelevant or inappropriate? If you don't immediately know the answer to these questions, try to find out.

If you provide content in a structure they understand or see is pertinent to their needs, they will be interested.

For example, if you are writing a presentation about new meeting room facilities, a talk to senior managers might briefly cover the costs and benefits, while a presentation to administration staff would provide more detail on how to use the rooms – like booking arrangements, and audiovisual equipment.

As well as thinking about content, ask yourself what language does your audience understand and expect? If you are using technical words or jargon will it be confusing for them? Will they expect you to be very respectful and formal, or more relaxed and casual?

Think about the different types of presentation you could make and how you would pitch them. Opening a discussion at your sports club about arrangements for a Christmas party is probably going to be breezier than a sales pitch to a major client for a £500,000 contract for a new security system.

How do I structure a presentation?

Step 1 – Think

Put some time aside to think, when you won't be interrupted and can concentrate on the task. After you are clear about the objective of the presentation, write down everything you think should be covered. It is sometimes helpful to do this as a mind map. Get a large sheet of blank paper and write down ideas randomly as they occur to you, then draw links between them with a different coloured pen.

Now organise the ideas. Decide which ones are logically linked together. Regroup the information – link the points which begin together, and arrange them in a sequence that makes sense. Here is an example:

> You are asked to give a presentation to another department on new meeting room facilities.

What is the objective?

> So all members of staff can make use of the rooms and know the booking procedures after the presentation.

Jot down your initial ideas:

> Security   Coffee/refreshments   Booking calendar
> Seating plan   Projectors   Air-conditioning
> Computer cabling   Location

Then start to organise them – more ideas will appear:

Booking procedure	**Demonstration facilities**
Booking number	Projectors and overheads
Ordering refreshments	Microphones
Security	Flipcharts and whiteboards
Order form	Computer cabling
Calendar and cancellations	Seating plan
Room location	**Housekeeping**
Reception area	Air-conditioning
Floor plans	Lighting controls
Fire exits	Telephones

Step 2 – Research

By this stage you have probably identified some areas where you don't have all the information you need. For instance, what are the health and safety regulations? How will telephone messages be handled? Do some research – read the appropriate material, or ask colleagues for information until you have notes on all the points to cover.

Step 3 – Outline your talk

Create a structure or storyboard for your presentation. Like a written report you will need to start with an introduction, cover the main points or arguments individually, and end with a conclusion.

A useful trick is to get a blank sheet of paper and divide it into squares, then write down a main message in each box. The initial aim is to organise the messages well.

This storyboard uses the meeting room example:

Introduction New meeting room facilities at Big Company plc	The company has set up new meeting rooms • Why? • What for?	The following rooms are available… *details*
The facilities offered are… *details*	*(More facilities)*	This is how to book a room… *details*
Before the meeting • organise security • clearance • refreshments	How to handle problems on the day	**Conclusion** Use the booking procedure Contact X for help

You may find that not all the squares get used, or more space is needed. It will depend on the complexity of the information you are trying to get across and the time you have available.

When you have a structure that is balanced and logical it is easy to begin the detailed work of writing the presentation and preparing visual aids. Each box is a 'main point'. Start to organise your material into secondary points under each heading until you have the full content of the presentation listed. Make sure all your secondary points support the main heading.

Which of the following has a better structure?

Meeting room facilities
Room 1
  seats 15 to 30
  projectors and video
Room 2
  seats 50 to 75
  projector and video
  microphones...

Booking arrangements
Reservation diary
Request forms
Telephone messages
Disabled access...

✔   ✘

Remember to keep your audience in mind all the time. If you have organised your ideas well, and use words they understand, they will grasp what you are saying much more easily, so will be more likely to pay attention.

What about using speaker's notes?

Why prepare speaker's notes in the first place? Well, it's a very unusual person who can stand up in front of a group and speak effortlessly on complex subjects without some notes.

However well you know the material, or have memorised and practised a speech, well-constructed notes are the best insurance policy. Think of the professionals – have you ever seen a politician, TV presenter, teacher or bestman at a wedding start talking without some pages or cards to refer to?

There are many different ways of preparing notes, and they will depend on the content and type of presentation.

In some cases presentations are written out in full as a script and read from paper or a screen autocue. Political speeches, press statements and technical presentations at conferences are often delivered in this way because precise wording is very important.

But reading from a written text can be extremely dull for the listener unless the speaker is highly trained. For most business presentations it is more important for the speaker to seem fluent, using words and phrases that come naturally. Structured notes that summarise the points to be made linked to slides or other visual aids are the key tool. They will prevent you from forgetting points or losing the sequence of ideas. You can also include symbols to indicate emphasis, and notes of examples or illustrations that make the presentation come alive for the listener.

If you are worried you might suddenly dry up in the middle of your presentation, and forget what you are saying, you can take the full text as a back-up. Keep calm, find your place on your script, and read the presentation until you feel comfortable with your notes again.

Everyone develops their own particular techniques for notes. A really effective way of learning how to do presentations well is to ask colleagues or friends who are good at presentations to show you their notes. See what ideas they use.

How do I create my notes?

There are three techniques commonly used for making up speaker's notes.

1. Create full pages of structured notes.
2. Create the overhead slides of the presentation and write notes on them. (Many computer software packages offer this facility.)
3. Write out index cards which can be held in one hand.

What ever method you choose:

❏ The writing must be clear and easy to read at a glance. It can be embarrassing for the speaker or distracting for the audience to get a word wrong or break off mid-sentence to decipher a squiggle. ('The virginal members of the team were… Oh, sorry, I meant original…')

❏ Each set of ideas should be captured on a single page or card. You should be able to get a mental picture of the main points at one glance.

❏ Each page should be single sided and numbered in order – just imagine dropping your notes seconds before you start to speak. If they have been numbered they can quickly be re-ordered.

❏ Ideally, pages should be bound in a way that makes them easy to turn so they will lie flat. Index cards could have a hole punched and be linked with a ring or treasury tag. Pages of notes in a ringbinder on a lectern or table will turn easily. Stapled pages or pages on clipboards have a tendency to bounce back, and should be avoided.

To start to build your notes take the presentation structure you have created – your storyboard – and try talking it. Speech is very different from writing and you will quickly find that to make it sound interesting you will need to add in pauses, questions, illustrations, summaries and links between your main points.

TIP A good presentation starts with a strong introduction – who you are, what the purpose of the presentation is and the material you will be covering. By setting an agenda or table of contents in the minds of your audience they will be more receptive to listening to detail – knowing that their questions or particular areas of interest will be dealt with.

Only experienced speakers can talk from copies of their slides alone (See section on golden rules for slides on page 18), so capturing emphasis and extras is the basis of speaker's notes.

The following technique is widely used for speaker's notes. Take a sheet of paper and divide it into three columns – the centre column should be the widest. Each column is for different components of your notes.

❑ Use the lefthand column to show the subject or point you are making and the visual aid to be used.

❑ Use the middle column to write down key points

❑ Use the righthand column to note links and illustrations

Keep plenty of space free for amendments and additions.

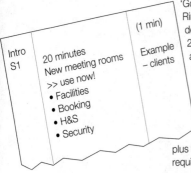

'Good morning, my name is Wanda Ringstar, from the building services department. Today I am going to take 20 minutes of your time to tell you about our new meeting rooms, so you will be able to use them straight away! For example, I know there are some important client presentations coming up. I'll be covering the facilities available, booking arrangements, plus the health and safety and security requirements.'

You can use highlighter pens and symbols to show where you want to add emphasis. Sometimes it is useful to include timings, and optional material which you can add in or leave out depending on the time available.

All of the information on the page could also be annotated on copies of your slides or on index cards.

How long should a presentation be?

Timing is very important. Audiences react badly if presentations last longer than the time allotted, or seem to be either drawn out or rushed.

Two things determine the length of a presentation – the time you are given and the complexity or volume of information to get across. A good rule of thumb is a minimum of two minutes per slide or major point. If the amount of time is fixed you may need to edit your presentation to fit the time available.

When you have decided on your structure, find a private room, and talk though the material out loud and time how long it takes. Remember speaking takes three to four times longer than reading. You will quickly find areas that you need to concentrate on and improve. (See the section on practising, page 23.)

3. How do I prepare visual aids?

Visual aids dramatically increase the impact of a presentation. If your audience both sees and hears information they are much more likely to remember it.

There are many types of visual aids to use – so think carefully and choose the ones most appropriate for your messages, as well as the size of the room, the facilities available, and your audience. Used badly visual aids can be time wasting and distracting. They can cause frustration for the audience if they can't be seen, or leave a poor impression if they aren't relevant or well prepared.

What type of visual aid equipment can I use?

Overhead projectors (OHPs) with acetate slides

OHPs are designed for presentations and can be used for small and large groups in normal lighting. The speaker faces the audience and manipulates the slides while the image is projected behind or above him or her.

It's possible to reveal points one at a time by using a mask (a sheet of paper) and drawing it down the page. It takes practice to use OHPs with panache, and it is very important to check visibility to ensure that the slides are legible, and that you don't stand in a position that blocks the view of the screen.

15

The advantage of OHPs is that they are simple, so in theory there is very little to go wrong with them, as long as you get the visibility right. However, as with *all* electrical or electronic equipment, make sure it works first!

35mm slide projectors

Photographic slides are loaded into a projector magazine that the speaker can operate with a remote control. Slides produce very colourful high-quality visuals and are particularly useful if photographs can be used to illustrate the information. For best results the room must be darkened – so other types of visual aid cannot be used at the same time. The disadvantages are that this type of slide can be expensive to produce, and they are easy to lose, damage or muddle. There's nothing more time wasting that trying to get slides in order, in the dark, in the middle of a talk.

Computer generated presentations

Computer generated presentations are now widely used in businesses. Slides are created in software packages and projected from the computer directly on to a screen. Additional features like moving objects, transitions and point-by-point build up of a list make them visually stimulating. Another advantage is that there are no production costs, and material can be edited and changed right up to the last minute. However, there are some disadvantages – if the equipment doesn't work properly, or the slides are badly done, the speaker can appear unprofessional or incompetent.

TIP If you are using slides, overhead projectors or computer generated presentations, keep in mind that most people are visually sophisticated. We are used to seeing well-designed brochures, and clever screen presentations on television. Lists of words on a screen will not have any impact.

Good layout, effective use of graphical devices like colour and shapes, plus diagrams, will help your audience remember the points you make. Above all the presentation must be readable and easy to understand.

Videos

Videos can be very useful to show how things are done – they can demonstrate complex processes and 'real life'. Consequently they are used extensively in training courses.

If you are going to use a video or video clip as part of your presentation make sure it is relevant – both to the subject and the audience. Time exactly how long the clip will take. Are the messages in it strong enough to devote that much time to? Test the equipment well beforehand so it can start smoothly. Your audience will quickly lose patience if a presentation stops for an operation on the equipment!

Physical props

Using props and examples as part of your presentation can capture interest very effectively. For instance, if you wanted to illustrate 'information overload' pulling a large pile of papers and magazines into view makes a strong point. Showing examples of new designs or materials next to previous ones fixes the changes in the viewer's mind very strongly. Think of the classic cooking programmes – with 'here's one I prepared earlier' – it's so much easier to understand how the recipe works if the stages of preparation can be illustrated visually.

Physical props won't work in very large groups though, because the people at the back won't see and so won't be able to get the message.

Handouts

Sometimes speakers give handouts of their presentation slides or speech to members of the audience to follow or write notes on during the speech. This is dangerous, as the temptation is to fast-forward by reading the document rather than pay attention to the speaker. It is sometimes better to give out material after the presentation, or as you use them if time and audience size allow for the interruptions.

Whiteboards

Many offices have laminated boards that can be written on with non-permanent coloured pens (make sure you have the right pens or you could damage the board permanently). They are very useful for building up messages in small groups and seminars as they are more interactive – you can respond to the audience and note points they make.

Whiteboards should not be used in formal presentations. It is time-consuming for the speaker to write, and eye contact is lost with the audience.

Flipcharts

There are two uses for flipcharts. The first is for prepared sheets used to present to small groups of people – slides on paper. These have the advantage of being more intimate – you can sit around a table with your audience rather than at a distance from them.

Secondly, empty flipcharts can be used like whiteboards, to write points as you progress. However, they are best used to capture the important points of a group discussion, or illustrate the answer to a question, rather than as a main presentation tool.

The most commonly used visual aids for presentations are projectors: OHPs, 35mm slide projectors and computer displays using special projectors called Barcos, which enlarge and project the image on a screen. If you are going to create a visual presentation, make sure that the equipment you will need is available and the room is arranged well for visibility.

How do I create an effective slide presentation?

To create the material software packages such as Freelance and Powerpoint are easy to learn and have standard templates that help design. The finished presentation can be output to paper, used to create acetates or 35mm slides, or projected direct from a computer.

The software packages will allow you to create diagrams and charts. They have useful additional features for writing speaker's notes, and creating handouts.

Here are some golden rules for creating slides:

❑ Design your slides in a horizontal frame and use a standard format and colour scheme throughout.

❑ Keep the colours, fonts (typefaces) and background constant so the audience isn't distracted by changes. Use two to four colours only. (Research has shown that the most legible slides for projection have a plain dark blue background with yellow or white writing.)

❑ Text is best presented in a numbered or bullet point list. This helps the audience get a mental picture of different ideas. A maximum of six lines of text per slide is recommended.

❑ Make sure every page has a title, and communicates a single idea.

❑ Keep the number of words to a minimum – write headings not sentences and use the largest typesize possible.

❑ Test, test, test legibility in the meeting place well before your presentation – in case you need to change the design.

How should I present charts and diagrams?

Tables, charts, graphs and diagrams are very powerful tools – much stronger than plain text – for presenting factual or statistical information and emphasising its significance. Think about the graphics that are shown on TV news programmes. Presenters cleverly get across complex information in a few seconds.

Each type of graphic has a specific use:

Tables	Display a large amount of data in a way that makes comparison easy.
Graphs	Illustrate trends in continuous information.
Charts	Barcharts and piecharts show discrete information about different types of things.
Diagrams	Are used to show non-statistical information – like structures or processes.

Here are some examples.

Tables

Who buys our haircare products?

Age Range	Product A Colorant	Product B Styling gel	Product C Glitter
Under 20s	2%	50%	98%
20–45	66%	45%	2%
Over 45	32%	5%	0%

The table allows comparison of three different products, in three different age groups.

Graphs

Sales of Styling Gel have increased dramatically in the last two months.

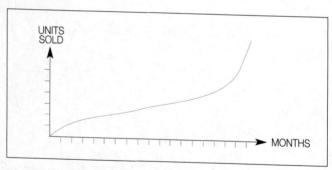

The graph indicates a trend and change over time.

Barcharts

Total sales are mixed.

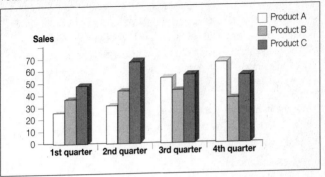

The barchart compares similar information on three different items.

Diagrams

This diagram shows the structure of activities – it isn't presenting statistical information. Try to describe it in words. How many sentences do you need to use?

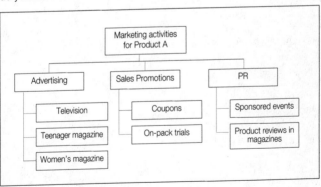

Using diagrams and charts will help you get complex messages across quickly if you learn how to use them well.

What about handouts?

Depending on the type of presentation you are making, different handouts may be appropriate to support your message and objectives. A copy of your slides may not be the best handout. If you are summarising very complex material then more detailed documents will be better. Here are some examples of supporting information you would use in different types of presentation.

Provide information or background

It is likely that your presentation will summarise key messages – handouts should provide more detail, for example:

❑ A detailed report
❑ Summary of statistics
❑ List of contact numbers or web pages.

Instruct or explain

Teaching or 'how to' material may be useful after a training or introduction course, such as:

❑ Guidance booklets or manuals
❑ Checklists or help cards
❑ Training course notes.

Persuade or convince

If you are 'selling' an idea or product, material that reinforces your message and offers more detail might be appropriate, for example:

❑ A sales brochure
❑ A request card
❑ Copies of favourable press coverage
❑ Credentials of key people.

4. How I prepare myself for a presentation?

How do I practise speaking clearly?

Once you have determined the content of your presentation, it's time to work on delivery. Reading from a set script – unless you are a highly trained presenter – will appear false and stilted. Expecting to be able to pick up a set of notes and talk fluently immediately is completely unrealistic. The best presenters know their material well and practise their presentations.

Of course enthusiasm for the subject counts for a lot. You will never engage an audience if you are half-hearted about the messages you are delivering. But structuring sentences so they are easy to understand and flow takes practice.

> 'Then you should say what you mean,' the March Hare went on. 'I do' Alice hastily replied 'At least – at least I mean what I say – that's the same thing you know!'
>
> 'Not the same thing a bit!' said the Hatter. 'Why you might just as well say that "I see what I eat" is the same thing as "I eat what I see"!'
>
> Lewis Caroll, *Alice's Adventures in Wonderland* 1865

Step 1

Once you have developed a set of notes and some draft visual aids, go into a private room and speak the presentation from start to finish. If possible record or video it. Notice the areas you feel uncomfortable about – where you stop or stutter. Listen to the flow of your talk – is it logical? Do you have a good introduction and strong conclusion?

Step 2

Go back through the presentation section by section and rephrase your points speaking aloud. Note down phrases you think are powerful, and revise your speaker's notes. This is a creative process – so don't try to do it in a hurry.

To get the timing right you will need to practise the presentation several times. Stand in front of a mirror and practise making direct eye contact with yourself. Watch how you appear.

Step 3

Get feedback – practise in front of a colleague or friend. A live audience will really help.

Go back through steps 1–3 until you feel comfortable, then go to the room where the presentation will be held, or similar venue, and do it again. Talk to the back of the room, talk to the front row. Practise using the equipment and showing your visual aids.

What should I wear?

A neat and tidy appearance is crucial if you want your presentation to be taken seriously. Good grooming means looking after every aspect of your appearance – hair, nails, and personal hygiene – as well as your choice of clothes and accessories.

Remember that as the presenter you want to be the centre of attention – but you don't want your appearance to be distracting. Inappropriate hairstyles, clothes or accessories may stop your audience listening to the words you are saying. People have different tastes, but it stands to reason that you won't keep their attention long once the audience has caught sight of neon pink socks with your sandals, the top of your underpants above your trousers, or a bra that shines through your blouse under a fluorescent light.

Of course your choice of outfit will depend very much on your audience, and the dress codes they have. Wearing the right clothes for your audience and profession, and feeling comfortable about your appearance, will enhance your confidence.

In office-based jobs, standard business dress for men is a suit and tie, with a plain coloured shirt and dark shoes. In the city or professional firms dark suits or pinstripes are expected. In media or advertising companies less formal coloured suits or jackets and trousers are often worn. For women the choices are broader – a suit or a skirt and jacket is always acceptable. Tailored dresses are frequently worn; and in most companies trousers for women is not a contentious issue.

You may wear a uniform at work, which makes the choice easier, but do ensure it is clean and ironed. Even if you normally wear casual clothes and so do your colleagues, making an effort to appear a bit more formal will help your audience take your presentation seriously.

Pay attention to details like polished shoes, tidy hair that doesn't flop in your eyes, unladdered tights etc. People will be distracted by things that look wrong or out of place and will stare at the egg stain on your tie rather than concentrate on what you're saying. Many presenters consciously choose outfits or accessories that draw attention to their faces – contrasting colours, vivid ties for men, or necklaces and earrings for women.

Wear clothes that are comfortable and won't restrict your movements or breathing – it's probably not the day to wear that jacket which is a flattering colour but just a bit too small. And avoid wearing anything that makes a noise – jewellery that jangles, loose change in pockets, shoes that squeak, clothes that rustle – they may distract you and inevitably will be picked up and amplified by any microphones.

Before you stand up or enter the room, check everything is in place or done up – collars, cuffs, zips, buttons, pocket linings etc.

How should I stand and move?

The first rule is – move! A rigid glassy-eyed presenter fixed by invisible wires to the floor and lectern is distressing for most audiences – no one likes to see a trapped animal. The more natural and normal you can appear the more relaxed your audience will be. Here are some tips.

❑ Stand with your feet slightly apart for balance – you will be able to move your arms and upper body easily, without looking strained.

❑ Look at the audience as much as possible. Move your head to scan the gathering so they know you are paying attention to them. This helps to build rapport, and makes you appear more confident and professional. If you just fix on one individual or a corner of the room the group will feel left out. By scanning you will also be able to get feedback on how the presentation is going.

❑ Use your hands to emphasise points – it's what we all expect in conversations and presentations are no different. One hand in a pocket can appear casual and relaxed. Two hands tucked away implies lack of interest in your subject verging on boredom. Point to your visual aids to underline key messages.

❑ If possible and you are confident enough, walk around a bit – movement keeps your audience's attention. If you do want to move around the room it can be helpful to have a colleague operate your visual aids – changing slides on a signal, so you don't have to worry about them. This will need practice beforehand to get the timing right.

❑ Don't fidget with your notes, clothing, hair or props. As the centre of attention everyone present will pick up on your unnecessary movements, and assume they are caused by nervousness. Gripping a pen or pointer in your hand can stop finger fiddling.

5. How should I prepare the room?

Presentations can take place in all kinds of rooms – from fixed lecture theatres, to classrooms, to smaller meeting rooms. Whatever type of room, it's essential to check beforehand:

❑ There are the right number of seats (with a few extra) for the size of the audience.

❑ There is a lectern or table for the speaker or speakers to stand and control the visual aids, with a place for notes.

❑ All seats can see the speaker, and the visual aids to be used. If it is not possible to move furniture around, try to determine before a presentation the best place to stand, and mark the seats that have poor visibility.

❑ The equipment – microphones and speakers, projectors, screens and controls – are all in place and in working order.

❑ You know how to work the lights, curtains, and temperature controls.

❑ There is no disturbing noise from outside the room likely to interfere with the presentation – for instance building work, heavy traffic, an office move, choir practice or a noisy kitchen.

❑ You know the health and safety requirements in case of an accident, or a fire alarm.

In a classroom or lecture theatre style room it is best to stand to one side of the screen so you don't block the audience's view of visual materials.

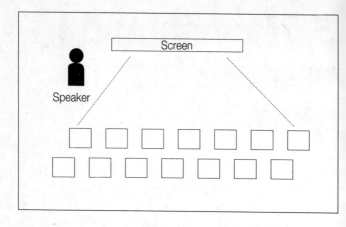

If you are making a presentation to a meeting, the seating plan is likely to be around a table or in a circle. Position the speaker's station at the head of the table furthest from the door. When they enter the room your audience will immediately understand a presentation will be taking place, and will choose a seat to see the show. Anyone arriving late or leaving early won't disrupt the session by walking infront of the presenter or screen.

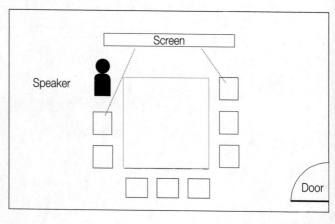

What about refreshments?

There are no strict rules about when it is appropriate to offer refreshments. Your organisation may have its own guidelines. Generally if you have invited visitors from outside your office or organisation it is polite to offer coffee or tea. If the presentation is to members of your own organisation and it is set to last not more than an hour, organising refreshments is not necessary.

If a room is set out in lecture theatre style (eg chairs but no tables are provided for the audience) then coffees and teas during the presentation will be difficult to handle, so allow time before the presentation starts for people to finish their drinks. If the room is set out as a classroom or a meeting room then cups can be placed on tables or desks and will not cause noise or inconvenience.

6. How do I handle an audience well?

It's very unlikely you will be asked to present to a group of people who have been physically forced into the room and tied to their chairs to stay. You may have a couple of reluctant attendees, but audiences are generally open to benefit from a presentation. They do expect to be respected and not have their time wasted.

You need to look and act professional. You must know your material well and, more importantly, be able to relate to their views and objectives. You need to hold their attention and make it easy for them to understand what you are saying.

How do I get the audience's attention?

What you say and do first creates a lasting impression. If your manner is confident as you introduce yourself, and you begin by saying something that captures attention and builds rapport, you will have established interest.

There are quite a few techniques that can be used:

1. State the subject and title of your talk, and summarise the objectives or material you will cover.

   'Team moral is a big issue for all of us, so today I am going to talk about three specific initiatives.'

   This is a fairly dry way to start, but the audience knows exactly what to expect. Or, do something that gets more notice…

2. Pose a question – it can be real or rhetorical.

   'How many of us had difficulty getting out of bed this morning?'

   The audience should start thinking about their own experience immediately and wonder if specific individuals will be questioned.

3. Provide some news that they will want to know.

   'I have just been told that sales last month were 3% higher than forecast – so our bonuses are confirmed.'

   (Now that is exciting!)

4. Use a quotation that links to the topic you are presenting – here is one for giving presentations in a confident manner. Stanley Kubrick said:

   'If you can talk brilliantly about a problem, it can create the consoling illusion that it has been mastered.'

5. Tell a story or anecdote…

   'I was sitting on the bus when…'

6. Start with some shared history

   'We all remember the last office move.'

7. Recount an interesting fact.

   'According to our records the average employee uses 11 post-it pads, 27 biros and 8 pencils a year.'

8. Make a dramatic statement.

   'All of you in this room could be carrying lethal viruses.'

9. Tickle their curiosity with something way off beam.

   'There are 107 ways of cooking eggs.'

Once you've got their attention, get to the main point quickly before interest begins to wander.

How do I keep the audience with me?

If you have worked hard to get the structure and content of your presentation right for your audience, how you deliver the talk will determine their attention span.

In the first few minutes you should aim to describe the topic or objective, and explain what you will be covering. It is also important to establish relevance – ie the specific need your listeners have which you will address – so that they pay attention and identify with what you say. Somehow you must link the presentation to their experience and provide some proof that the time taken to listen is worthwhile.

> 'I'm sure we would all like to reduce the amount of time spent dealing with irrelevant telephone calls. This morning I will introduce some practice guidelines aimed to do just that. These guidelines have already been piloted in one office and have resulted in a time saving of one hour per person per week.'

The single most important thing to convey is enthusiasm for the subject. If you are smiling, radiating energy and 'full on' its very difficult for anyone listening not to become engaged. Insincerity can be spotted a mile off though – so don't just act sincere – be it!

Language

You need to think consciously about how you will build rapport and get listeners to associate with you. The choice of personal pronouns, and open acknowledgement of issues they face helps. For example,

> 'We all feel the burden of heavy administrative processes during the working day.'

conveys more empathy than

> 'You have heavy administrative processes to deal with.'

Your choice of words is very important. The simpler the words and sentence structure you use the better. Avoid jargon and unnecessary figures of speech. Beware of vague statements or words that can be misinterpreted.

'Essentially the concept is one of continuous improvement and gradual step changes in performance. Furthermore, the impact can be identified and quantified in a very short space of time.'

✖

'The approach is to make small changes in performance continuously. Improvements can be measured within four weeks.'

✔

Practise using phrases, and test alternatives to see if there is a clearer way of expressing an idea. Are the words you have chosen strong and definite enough, or might they be too aggressive for your listeners? Is the nuance right?

'This project has the chairman's backing, and we are confident it will proceed.'

'The chairman is driving this project, so failure is not an option.'

Colourful comparisons or similes will grab wandering attention.

'Deliveries in reception are proving more dangerous obstacles for visitors than a Gladiators contest.'

Nonverbal feedback

Be aware of your audience – look out for the nonverbal feedback – are they looking at you and nodding as points are made? Or is there a lot of movement in the room, the noise of rustling and side conversations taking place and obvious doodling or note-passing?

If the audience gets very restless, it probably means there is disagreement or lack of acceptance in what you are saying, so they stop listening. To recover the situation you can either build in reassurances:

'Meeting these new targets may sound as arduous and impossible as swimming the channel, but I assure you it's much more like walking along the top of the White Cliffs of Dover.'

Or stop and ask for input – 'Is anyone not comfortable with this?' If you don't acknowledge that the group is sending a signal when it becomes obvious the likelihood of regaining attention is minimal.

Closing

End the presentation by summarising the key points, and always finish on a high point – a strong sentence and upbeat statement.

> 'I'm sure when you have reviewed our proposal to set up a sports club for the over 80s you will decide to make the £3,000,000 investment.'

How do I use my voice well?

First – make sure you can be heard! You will generally need to speak louder and more slowly than normal, to ensure that you can be heard clearly. Project your voice to the furthest part of the room. This can feel a bit unnatural – particularly if nerves have set in. Inhale deeply to start; this will calm you.

Be very careful to pronounce words clearly – almost over-emphasise difficult syllables. Watch out that you don't mumble the ends of words or confuse Fs with Ss. Never cover your mouth while speaking – try to keep your hands away from your face entirely.

There are many ways to use your voice like a musical instrument when giving a speech. You can alter the pitch, tone and speed, and add emphasis to accent the message you are trying to get across.

It's a good idea to pause frequently. This technique can be used to let a point sink in and it also allows you to draw breath, look for feedback and concentrate on the next point.

Make sure there is some water and a glass nearby in case your throat becomes dry. Don't suck sweets or chew gum because you won't be able to speak clearly with anything in your mouth (but your chewing and sucking noises will be very audible).

Practise changing the tone, pitch and emphasis of key phrases until you are happy with the effect.

> *I* really feel this is important
> I *really feel* this is important
> I really feel this is *important*

How can I use humour?

Humour is a great tool to use in a presentation. It helps to change mood or lighten up if you have covered very complex material. It can help to establish empathy with the group. But you must get it right for those you are addressing. There are a few points to bear in mind.

1. Humour needs to be related to the subject. Any old joke or quip will be out of place and make your subject seem disjointed.

2. Don't expect to generate huge belly laughter or mass hysterical giggling. A smiling group will be receptive to your messages.

3. It's important to be brief. Appropriate quotes and similes are the best vehicles to introduce humour into the overall context of what you are saying.

4. 'War stories' – for example, of similar experiences with amusing outcomes – can draw the group to you. People like hearing about disaster and others' embarrassment!

5. Think of the type of people in the group – what will they find funny?

6. Avoid the danger zones for political correctness – references to religion, politics, race and sex can generate extreme reactions.

7. Avoid 'insider' jokes unless you are sure that the whole audience will understand them, and be drawn together by their use.

What if I get interrupted?

The most important point about interruptions is not to ignore them or compete with them. If you try to appear oblivious your audience will become more interested in where your breaking point will be than what you are saying. There are two types of interruptions that can occur:

❑ Physical interruptions – accidents, people entering or leaving the room, strange noises, pagers or mobile phones ringing, or problems with equipment.

❑ Questions – which will be dealt with in the next section.

So, if an accident occurs – acknowledge it to the group, decide whether to carry on, or take a break. Calmly tell the audience what is happening, and then restart with energy. It can be an opportunity for humour!

For example

A fly keeps landing on your overhead projector slide, like a random bouncing ball on the screen, and it captivates the audience. You can acknowledge the insect by saying...

> 'Excuse me, ladies and gentlemen, my small assistant seems to have lost the plot – does anyone object to capital punishment?'

...then kill it.

Or

Catering staff turn up with a loud clattering trolley of cups. The noise and movement and anticipation of refreshments will distract your audience, so take a break.

> 'Perhaps this would be a good time to pause for refreshment – and I will start again in 10 minutes when we have all had tea.'

Or

A dramatic thunderstorm breaks outside the window.

> 'Look's like I've been upstaged.'

> 'Divine intervention – time for a break.'

> 'Who has to walk home?'

> 'Someone is upset at not being invited to my talk today.'

How do I handle questions?

If the question is an interruption, it's a good idea to buy some time to think. The probability is high that a knee-jerk response will come out badly.

❑ Acknowledge the questioner – if you know the answer, talk to the questioner directly.

- ❑ Don't show that you are uncomfortable with the question – stay calm.

- ❑ Summarise or repeat back the question, so the rest of the audience understands what you are dealing with.

- ❑ Provide a brief answer – don't be tempted into a long explanation which you haven't prepared for…

  'Thank you Hugh Liggen, perhaps I wasn't clear when I explained the meaning of an oxymoron as a figure of speech with pointed conjunction of apparent contradictions – a good example would be football culture.'

- ❑ Or mirror back…

  'What do *you* think oxymoron means?'

Questions *can* work to your advantage. You can use them to get feedback from the audience or to emphasise a point you want to make. There are different types of questions to handle:

- ❑ participants who are genuinely not following what you are saying
- ❑ participants who disagree with points you are making
- ❑ attention seekers, who have a different agenda.

If the question is relevant, use the audience – ask:

  'Is anyone else not clear on this point?'

  'Mr Wordsmith, you are an expert on this – perhaps you could provide an explanation?'

If the question isn't relevant you could say:

  'I don't think we have the time to explore that in detail in the limited time available – perhaps we could speak about it later.'

  'Thank you for your interesting comments – perhaps we could return to the central topic of this meeting.'

If you genuinely don't know the answer – say so, and offer to follow up:

  'I'm sorry, I don't have those figures with me. Perhaps I could investigate and get back to you tomorrow?'

7. Are there other types of presentation?

What are group presentations?

There are lots of good reasons to use more than one person in a long or complex presentation. You can involve experts in specific topic areas or have individuals presenting contrasting views. It will also make it more interesting for the audience.

Organisation and coordinated preparation are crucial to avoid the whole event appearing disjointed. Particular dangers are repetition of information, lack of logical links between sections, and different styles of visual aid or way of speaking to the audience. You can avoid these by one person creating the whole structure – or by collaboration. As most people are more comfortable and fluid at giving presentations they have written, it is crucial that everyone is involved.

❏ At the storyboard stage, when you are setting up the structure of the presentation, compare notes or agree an overall structure.

❏ When each person has written their section, get back together for a run through, to find overlaps and make sure the sections link.

❏ Practise together – ask other people to listen and comment.

What are sales presentations?

Sales presentations are specifically about persuading people to do business with you. They can be to groups of people from different organisations – or more commonly to a specific company.

The advantage of preparing a talk – rather than sending a brochure or making a telephone call – is the contact you are making. The opportunity to provide detailed information and respond to questions immediately is a very useful way of marketing complex or customised services.

You may not know a great deal about your audience, or any of their attitudes. Developing sensitive antennae to respond to their verbal and nonverbal signals is crucial. Of course presentation skills are covered in detail in most sales training courses, and depending on the business you work in different elements will be more or less appropriate.

There are three types of sales presentation:

❑ Launches or press announcements
❑ Introduction or credentials
❑ Specific proposal or pitch

Product launches or press conferences usually have a wide guest list and aim to get a large audience – so they are the least 'personal' type of presentation. Your aim is to get the audience interested in something which has not be available before, or offers great improvements on a previous product or service.

At introduction or credentials meetings your aim is to show how capable your organisation is. What skills and expertise are available, successful work with other clients, and the unique benefits you can offer. The objective is to get the audience to show interest in your product or service for their own organisation, and then to move on to the next stage – ask for a specific proposal, discuss costs and ordering process.

Generally a proposal or pitch presentation is responding to a brief – for instance an advertising campaign, a new computer system, a training programme, refurbishment of offices, or developing a website. Your talk should address what you plan to do to meet the requirements they set out, how you will approach the project and, crucially, how much it will cost.

8. What else should I think about?

What are some things to avoid?

When giving any type of presentation, there are some common sense rules of things not to do. Here is a list of 'don't do's – to avoid embarrassment!

✘ Don't have a late night before a presentation and over-indulge in spicy food, alcohol (or other substances) and under-indulge in sleep.

✘ Don't cut corners on travel time – make sure you arrive early with plenty of leeway for bad journeys or dealing with last-minute problems before the presentation. Remember, you'll need a few minutes to prepare the room and ensure all equipment is working.

✘ Don't start a presentation on an empty stomach – you will be aware of tummy growls, even if no one else can hear them.

✘ Don't drink carbonated drinks before or during your speech. Belching might detract from a professional impression.

✘ Don't have a heavy meal or too much to drink before you speak.

✘ Don't decide to change your presentation radically at the last minute.

✘ Don't forget the name of the person who is introducing you – write it on your notes.

How can I recover the situation when things go wrong?

Many unexpected events can happen in presentations – as in life – that at the time feel like the worst possible event. It's not really the end of the world, but perhaps it could have been avoided. Here is a case study that shows how important it is to be prepared, keep calm, and develop your own 'recovery techniques' for when things start going wrong.

Case study

Desmond Aster had a bad day. One of those days where giving a presentation – just a normal business activity – transformed itself in to a five-hour white-knuckle ride.

Des had arranged to give a presentation to colleagues from all over the country at the firm's central offices in London, about the new training course he had developed to help new recruits understand the company structure, and product lines. The meeting was set up several weeks in advance, the room was booked and travel arrangements were made.

Unfortunately… A week before the presentation Des fell off a ladder in a freak DIY accident and broke his arm.

Fortunately… Most of his notes and visual aids were already drafted, so he asked a colleague to help him do the final preparation. He also didn't need to drive to the meeting, as he had found he could travel more quickly by train and had already bought his tickets to avoid queuing on the day.

Unfortunately… The train he caught had technical defects and was taken out of service at Watford.

Fortunately… Des had caught an early train to allow plenty of time, and could catch the next service without worrying about being late.

Unfortunately… When Des arrived at the offices the meeting room didn't have the right number of chairs and tables and the computer projection equipment wasn't working.

Fortunately… Des had requested the telephone number of the office services department in case of problems, and a great chap called Malcolm Tent turned up to rearrange the room.

Unfortunately… Des and Malcolm couldn't get the computer projection system to work at all.

Fortunately… Des had a back up – he had prepared overhead projection slides of his presentation. Malcolm set up the overhead projector because Des couldn't lift it.

Unfortunately… Some of the attendees arrived before the official start of the presentation.

Fortunately… Des had worked out this might happen as people were travelling from all over the country and had arranged for coffee and biscuits to be available in the reception area.

Unfortunately… At the designated start time 30% of the audience had not arrived.

Fortunately… Des had allowed for a late start in the presentation and had planned to use the first minutes getting the audience to introduce themselves to each other. He also had the foresight to ensure their were empty chairs at the back of the room to avoid disruption from late arrivals.

Unfortunately… Des realised he couldn't talk effectively and replace slides on the OHP with only one arm.

Fortunately… He knew that bathos was incredibly powerful so he asked for assistance from the audience – a volunteer to change his slides. The audience thought this was endearing and the volunteer was a good sport.

Unfortunately… The volunteer had a mobile phone which started to ring during the presentation.

Fortunately… Des had a line – he took the phone and said, 'Hello, nice of you to call Prime Minister, but I am on a stage with 50 people looking at me – can this wait? The audience laughed and Des was able to say, 'I think it would be a good idea if everyone turned of their phone and pagers so we don't discriminate against the Prime Minister.'

Unfortunately… The person who had developed the previous course, Marty Pants, was in the audience, and decided to ask difficult questions like 'Why wasn't more time spent explaining the company products in detail?'

Fortunately… Des had been expecting this question and explained that an exhibition and open days were being introduced as well to let new employees find out about the products relevant to them in more detail. He knew the quickest way to stop further interruptions was to involve the rest of the audience so he said, 'I would be very interested in everyone's opinion on this – do you think the induction presentation should just focus on the overall structure to keep the presentation short?' There was a general murmur of assent and a few murmurs of 'Shut up, Marty' which Des chose to ignore.

Unfortunately… At that point two shirtless window cleaners decided to abseil down the building and peer in to the room, while drinking a well-known brand of fizzy beverage.

Fortunately… Des kept his head, saying 'You see how difficult it is to keep a group of people concentrating for any length of time.' Because he had checked the room beforehand he knew where the controls were to shut the blinds and was able to block out his competitors.

Unfortunately… With all the interruptions the presentation was ten minutes behind schedule so Des had to decide what to cover in the last few minutes.

Fortunately… Des had prepared a summary slide and handouts for the audience to take away, so he was able to skip forward, present the conclusions and suggest that any questions could be asked in the break or by telephoning him after the event.

Unfortunately… Marty decided to go for one last difficult question.

Fortunately… The rattle of cups and aroma of fresh brewed coffee proved too much for the audience so they left.

So Des had to deal with a pile of problems which he never dreamed of when he agreed to do a presentation and started constructing his slides and speaker's notes. But because he did his preparation, and anticipated some likely problems, he was able to recover the situation, and get his message delivered.

What publications could I look at?

Go to the business section in your local library to find out what is available. There are many publications you can learn from, depending on your experience and knowledge. These are just a selection.

Making successful presentations, Patrick Forsyth, Sheldon Business Books

Presentation tips and techniques, Mike Levy, Wyvern Crest 1997

The complete idiot's guide to successful business presentations, Lin Kroeger, Alpha 1997

For advice on videos, you can contact Video Arts Ltd, 68 Oxford Street, London W1N 0L8

About the Author

Josy Roberts has worked in administrative, marketing and management roles over the last 15 years for a variety of organisations, including family-owned small businesses, charities and major corporations. As well as the scars of experience she holds an honours degree in Sociology, a marketing certificate and Diploma in Management.

She believes strongly that the success of organisations and individuals – whatever they do – is based on communications skills and a professional approach, and with that the working day can and should be enjoyable.

This first edition published in 1998 in Great Britain by Trotman and Company Limited, 12 Hill Rise, Richmond, Surrey TW10 6UA
© Trotman and Company Limited 1998

British Library Cataloguing in Publication Data
A catalogue record for this book is available from the British Library
ISBN 0 85660 327 9

Printed and bound in Great Britain by Redwood Books

Presentations

your questions and answers

Josy Roberts